World Book's Learning Ladders

What Living Things Need

WORLD
BOOK

a Scott Fetzer company
Chicago
www.worldbookonline.com

WORLD
BOOK

233 N. Michigan Avenue
Chicago, IL 60601
U.S.A.

For information about other World Book publications, visit our Web site at
http://www.worldbookonline.com or call 1-800-WORLDBK (967-5325).

For information about sales to schools and libraries, call 1-800-975-3250 (United States);
1-800-837-5365 (Canada).

Library of Congress Cataloging-in-Publication Data

What living things need.
    p. cm. -- (World Book's learning ladders)
    Summary: "Introduction to living things' basic needs
using simple text, illustrations, and photos. Features
include puzzles and games, fun facts, a resource list,
and an index"-- Provided by publisher.
    Includes index.
    ISBN 978-0-7166-7744-4
    1. Biology--Juvenile literature. 2. Life (Biology)--Juvenile
literature. I. World Book, Inc.
    QH309.2.W43 2011
    570--dc22
                                        2010026719

World Book's Learning Ladders
Set 2 ISBN: 978-0-7166-7746-8

Printed in China by Shenzhen Wing King Tong Paper Products Co., Ltd.
Shenzhen, Guangdong
1st printing December 2010

Editorial
    Editor in Chief: Paul A. Kobasa
    Associate Manager, Supplementary Publications:
        Cassie Mayer
    Writer: Karen Ingebretsen
    Editor: Brian Johnson
    Researcher: Cheryl Graham
    Manager, Contracts & Compliance
    (Rights & Permissions): Loranne K. Shields

Graphics and Design
    Manager: Tom Evans
    Coordinator, Design Development and Production:
        Brenda B. Tropinski
    Photographs Editor: Kathy Creech

Pre-Press and Manufacturing
    Director: Carma Fazio
    Manufacturing Manager: Steven Hueppchen
    Production/Technology Manager: Anne Fritzinger

Photographic credits: Cover: © Rick Parsons, Dreamstime; WORLD BOOK illustration by Q2A
Media; Shutterstock; p1, p3, p9, p10, p11, p16, p19, p26, p27, p29, p30: Shutterstock; p4,
p20: Masterfile; p6: Alamy Images; p12: SuperStock; p22: Getty Images

Illustrators: WORLD BOOK illustration by Q2A Media; WORLD BOOK illustration by Alex Ebel
and Robert Kuhn; WORLD BOOK illustration by Kate Lloyd-Jones, Linden Artists Ltd.

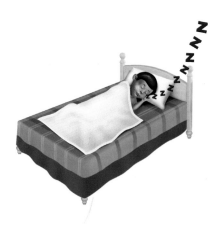

What's inside?

This book tells you about the needs of living things. Plants, animals, and people have different ways of meeting their needs.

The living world

Living things are things that are alive now. Living things can grow and change. Plants, animals, and people are living things. Nonliving things are things that never lived or are dead now. Rocks, houses, and cars are nonliving things.

Clouds are nonliving things.

Water is a nonliving thing.

What living and nonliving things can you find in this picture?

Trees and plants are living things.

It's a fact!
Earth is home to more than 10 million different kinds of living things.

Cars are nonliving things.

Human beings are living things.

Animals are living things.

Basic needs

All living things have basic needs, or things they need to stay alive. Almost all living things need food, water, air, and living space. This is true no matter where a thing lives. Plants, animals, and people each have some special needs, too.

Plants need sunlight to grow. Plants use energy in sunlight to make food.

Living things need **air**.

It's a fact!

Rain forests provide living space for more than half the world's different kinds of animals.

Some birds build nests in trees. The nest serves as **shelter** for their young.

The family who lives here grows **food** in this vegetable garden.

People, plants, and animals need **water**.

Food

Food gives people and animals energy to move about. It also gives your body the energy it needs to work. Plants do not need to eat, but they do need energy. They get their energy from sunlight.

Some people eat **meat** as part of their diet.

It's a fact!

People can live without food for more than two months. But they can live without water for only about a week.

JANUARY

SUN	MON	TUE	WED	THU	FRI	SAT
X	X	X	X	X	X	X
8	X	X	X	X	X	14
X	16	X	18	19	20	21
X	X	X	25	26	27	28
X	30					

Grass is an important plant to many hoofed animals. This cow gets the energy it needs from eating grass.

Bread is made from the **grains** of some plants. It helps the body process food.

Eating **fruits and vegetables** every day helps to keep the body healthy.

Water

We could not live without water. Water helps to move nourishing things through the body. It also helps the body get rid of wastes. Plants also need water to live and grow.

Many animals get water from streams or other sources of **fresh water.**

People need to **drink** lots of water when they exercise.

Plants take in most of their water from the **soil.**

Clouds are made of tiny droplets of water. Rain and snow fall from clouds.

Farmers need lots of water to grow crops. They use machines to water large fields.

It's a fact!

A jellyfish is made almost entirely of water.

Air

Air is made up of gases. One of these gases is oxygen. People and animals take in oxygen and give off the gas carbon dioxide. Plants do the opposite. They take in carbon dioxide and give off oxygen. People and animals depend on plants to give off oxygen.

We cannot see, smell, or taste air. But we can see things moved by the air.

On a cold day, you can see your **breath** when you breathe out.

It's a fact!
Most adults breathe 10 to 16 times a minute while awake and only 6 to 8 times per minute while sleeping.

Trees and other green plants exchange carbon dioxide for **oxygen**.

We can see chimney **smoke** drifting in the air when it's cold outside.

Animals and people need **air** to stay alive.

13

Let's go camping

When you plan a camping trip, you need to make sure that all your basic needs will be met. A tent will give you shelter. You can bring food and water with you. You don't need to worry about air—wherever you go, there will be air!

14

Where is the bird's nest?

Words you know

Here are some words that you read earlier in this book. Say them out loud, then try to find the things in the picture.

nest

water

cloud

food

tree

plant

Where is there fresh water?

Sunlight

Plants need sunlight to stay alive. Without sunlight, they could not make food. And if there were no plants, animals and people could not survive. The sun also warms the air. Without the sun, Earth would be too cold for us to live here.

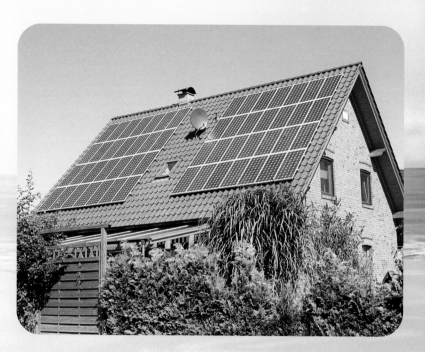

Some homes have special panels on the roof that collect energy from the sun. The energy is converted into electricity to power lights and other household items.

The **sun** is the star that is closest to Earth. It gives us light, heat, and other kinds of energy.

It's a fact!
The changing seasons are caused by the tilt of Earth as it moves around the sun.

Plants use energy from the sun to make food.

Lizards and other reptiles need sunshine to keep their bodies warm.

People need small amounts of sunlight to stay healthy. But too much sunlight is bad for your skin.

17

Shelter

Many animals need shelter to protect them from weather or attack. Some animals use caves for shelter. Others dig a hole in the ground. People need shelter, too. Shelters can be built from many kinds of materials.

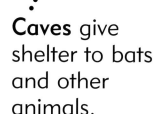

Caves give shelter to bats and other animals.

It's a fact!

Some people in Europe lived in caves as far back as 1 million years ago!

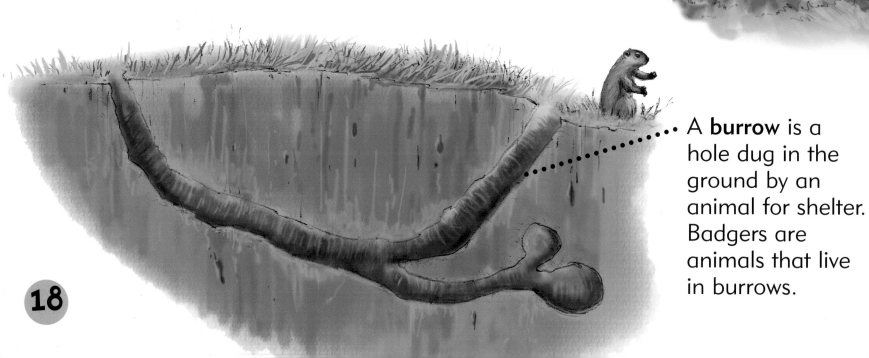

A **burrow** is a hole dug in the ground by an animal for shelter. Badgers are animals that live in burrows.

Polar bears dig their **dens** out of snow. The den protects them from cold temperatures.

Houses in many parts of the world are made of brick. Bricks are strong blocks made of baked clay.

Some houses are built on stilts (poles driven into the ground). This protects the house against flooding.

Living together

Many animals live in groups to meet their needs. A group can be as small as one pair. Some groups have thousands or even millions of members. Some animals live in groups to hunt. Others live in groups for protection from other animals.

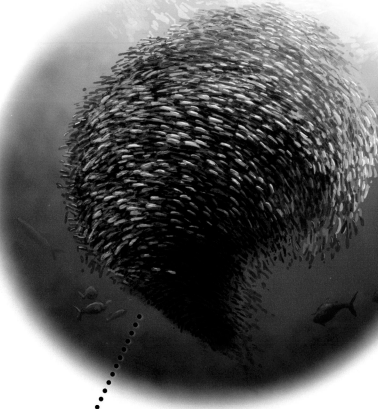

A group of fish is called a **school**. The fish gather into a ball when a hunter approaches. This makes it hard for the hunter to attack any one fish.

A group of lions is called a **pride**. Lions work together as a team to hunt.

It's a fact!

Gorillas live in family groups. One adult male called a silverback leads the group through the forest.

A group of honey bees lives in a **colony**. The bees work together to make food and take care of their young.

A group of elephants is called a **herd**. Elephants help each other watch for hunting animals.

A group of wolves is called a **pack**. The wolves work together to hunt other animals.

21

Web of life

All plants, animals, and people are connected. We call this connection the web of life. People and animals depend on plants for food. Plants also make the oxygen we breathe. In turn, animals help to spread seeds to make new plants. Plants also need the carbon dioxide people and animals breathe out.

Grass and other plants provide food for many animals.

People make rugs, clothing, and other household items out of plants.

Bees drink a sugary liquid from flowers. They also help to spread a special dust that plants need to make new plants.

The **sun** is at the center of the web of life. Animals and plants need the sun to survive.

Animals help to keep soil healthy. Their body waste gives the soil nourishing things that help new plants to grow.

Chickens provide us with eggs to eat. Many people also eat meat from chickens.

An afternoon in the park

It's a beautiful day to visit the park! People are watching the animals, and the animals are watching the people. Trees and flowers are blooming, and a gentle breeze blows.

24

Which living things produce oxygen?

Words you know

Here are some words that you learned earlier. Say them out loud, then try to find the things in the picture.

grass   sun   animal
bee   plant   shelter

Did you know?

Hummingbirds take in half their weight in food every day.

In the wild, elephants usually eat for about 16 hours a day.

Blue whales are the largest creatures that ever lived. But they eat very small animals called krill. Some krill are smaller than half an inch (1.3 centimeters) long!

Many useful medicines come from plants. Some of these plants have been used as medicines for hundreds of years.

A tomato is about 95 percent water.

Koalas that live in the wild rarely drink water. Instead, they get the water they need by eating the leaves of plants.

Puzzles

Close-up!

We've zoomed in on three scenes from this book. Can you tell which of the four basic needs are shown?

1

2

3

Double trouble!

These two pictures are not exactly the same. Can you find the five things that are different in picture b?

a

b

Answers on page 32.

Match up!

Match each word on the left with its picture on the right.

1. rabbit

2. nest

3. cloud

4. colony

5. burrow

6. flowers

a

b

c

d

e

f

Answers on page 32.

True or false

Can you figure out which of these statements are true? Turn to the page numbers given to help you find the answers.

Air is made up of only one gas. **Go to page 12.**

4

Clouds are living things. **Go to page 4.**

1

There are more than ten million kinds of living things on Earth. **Go to page 5.**

2

3

Plants take in carbon dioxide and give off oxygen. **Go to page 12.**

A jellyfish's body is made almost entirely of air. **Go to page 11.**

5

Answers on page 32.

Find out more

Books

Adaptation and Survival by Denise Walker (Smart Apple Media, 2007)
Information about how living things adapt to survive on Earth.

Elements in Living Organisms by Suzanne Slade (PowerKids Press, 2007)
Learn about the major building blocks of all living things on Earth.

Is It a Living Thing? by Bobbie Kalman (Crabtree Publishing, 2008)
How can you tell if something is living or nonliving? This book describes the features of living things and explains how they are dependent on nonliving things for survival.

Living and Nonliving by Carol Lindeen (Capstone Press, 2008)
This book explains the difference between living and nonliving things.

Snap! by Mick Manning and Brita Granström (Frances Lincoln Children's Books, 2006)
Learn about the food chain through this comical story.

Who Eats Who in City Habitats? by Robert Snedden (Smart Apple Media, 2007)
Read this book to learn about the food chain in a city habitat.

Web sites

Kind News Online!
http://www.kindnews.org/
A Web site that teaches children to respect and protect everything that natural things need to survive, sponsored by the Humane Society of the United States.

NBII Kids
http://kids.nbii.gov/
The National Biological Information Infrastructure created this Web site for kids, featuring interesting facts, stories, games, and activities that teach about living things.

Science Kids
http://www.sciencekids.co.nz/gamesactivities/plantsanimals.html
Find different kinds of living things in the picture and learn interesting facts about each.

The Web of Life
http://www.kidsplanet.org/wol/index.html
A spider tells a story about the web of life.

Answers

Puzzles
from pages 28 and 29

Close-up!
1. air   2. food   3. water

Double trouble!
In picture b, the trees on the left are missing, the horse's spots are reversed, the squirrel is facing the opposite direction, the fence is missing a rail, and the blue butterflies are missing.

Match up!
1. f
2. d
3. b
4. a
5. e
6. c

True or false
from page 30

1. false
2. true
3. true
4. false
5. false

Index